Go in Peace

Go in Peace

Poems by

Theodore McDowell

Cover design by Shay Culligan
Cover image by Wallace Henry on Unsplash
Author photo by Theodore McDowell

ISBN: 979-8-90146-816-6
Library of Congress Control Number: 2026935138

Kelsay Books
502 South 1040 East, A-119
American Fork, Utah 84003
Kelsaybooks.com

In loving memory of Rachel: my oldest sister,
my shaman, my best friend, and my only "Sis."
Your life was a gift,
and your story continues to inspire.
You will never be forgotten.

Wisdom (3:1–3, Revised Standard Version): But the souls of the righteous are in the hand of God, and no torment will ever touch them. In the eyes of the foolish they seemed to have died, and their departure was thought to be an affliction, and their going from us to be their destruction; but they are at peace."

Author's Note

I am indebted to Elisa Affanato for her skillful editing of this poetry collection. Elisa is a talented poet and editor.

Content Warning

The poems contained in this poetic memoir
explore the topics of child abuse and suicide.

Contents

The Bruises Turn into the Blues

Dad strangles the steering wheel,
bonfires in his eyes.
Flames scorch my soul.
I'm kindling wood
for the wrath of God.

I stare out the window.
Wheat fields stretch toward paradise,
untouched except by awe.
A white church with a bell tower
set on a hill
protects a weathered red farmhouse
with hay bales scattered
across the furrowed fields.

Window down,
sunrays magically transform
into stalks and kernels
bending in submission to the breeze.
Deep inhale of sun-soaked wheat.

Wind brushes my face
like Mom's hand
sweeping across my cheek.
A cloudless sky,
I crave the azure in her eyes.

Remembrance of Mom baking bread,
muscles relax into her warm voice.
My soft unfolding into the memory
feels gentle, maternal, and nurturing,
like the feminine side of God.

I glance at Dad,
sacred caresses turn dark, masculine,
violent. I roll up the window,
trying to forget
new bruises on my sister's arms.

How could the Creator
of wheat fields and church bells
allow Dad to beat his daughter
and shun his son?

How could the God
of haystacks and steeples
be indifferent to the abuse?

At home,
I flee the judgment of God,
sprint to Sis in her secret shelter
beside the river in the backyard.
She's smoking a cigarette
and drinking a beer
to take the edge off damnation.

I touch her bruises,
ask her how she survives.
She smiles and whispers:
the self-respect
of hopeless defiance.
The bruises slowly
turn into the blues.

Sis: My Shaman, My Best Friend

Growing up in the crucible of abuse,
addiction, and mental illness,
my oldest sister Rachel survived
by learning to see the world from odd angles.

She lived each day as if it were her first—
full of raw astonishment,
like Eve on the first morning,
waking to dew baptizing the earth.

We spent hours sitting on a river bank
in the woods behind our house.
Sis prepared me for the danger
and wonder of the world.

There would be evenings the trees
bruised the bank with shade.
There would also be moments
when the shadows transformed
into the calligraphy of God.

Sis spoke in metaphors.
The images were chisel marks
creating my rough-hewn identity.
Her words were soothing
as David's harp.
The layered meanings
were the modern parables
found in jazz improvisations
pouring tribulations and triumphs
from a horn.

My shaman's word pictures
were fragments of awe,
jolting me outside my ordinary existence:
water lilies reopening in the morning
at the Japanese garden
were steppingstones to Buddha's peace;
for her, the most beautiful sound
was the wind chanting the call to prayer
from minarets of trees.

One afternoon at a nature reserve,
she lowered her binoculars and exclaimed
that Great White Egrets taking flight
were the wings and wonder of death.

In her late teen years, Sis balanced
trauma and wisdom.
She knew tribulations and traumas
cremated the colors of joy.
And yet, the deepest truths
were the color of sackcloth and ashes
and could only be seen through tears.

Sis was a rebel with a bohemian style.
She thrived in coffee houses
and Blind Willie's Jazz Club,
listening to protest music
strummed on acoustic guitars.

For Sis, music was mystical.
Within an eternal hush, she listened
to the plucked strings of a gypsy guitar
tremble toward the stars.

One evening I caught her kneeling
beside her bed. She ruffled
my hair, explaining that prayer
was rebellion against despair.

Sis loved high-wire acts,
like the adrenaline rush of sneaking
out past curfew to meet a boy.
She spun folk wisdom to manage
the mystery and mirage of young love.

A first kiss lit votive candles in her eyes.
Attraction was more powerful
than the brutal pull
of the moon on ocean tides.
Lost love was shrapnel lodged
too close to the heart.

Sis possessed an artist's eye
for capturing the beauty and meaning
embedded in suffering and trauma.
Her brush was made from a splinter of the cross.
Her paintings caught fire, like torches
flaming in the catacomb-darkness of the world.

Her pencil etched the shadow-side of existence.

Looking back, I cherish most the afternoons
Sis taught me how to climb above danger
and rest in safe places.

We climbed an old Magnolia tree,
branch by branch,
rising from brown dirt
to untouched green leaves of spring,
branch by branch,
clasping at bark rough, gnarled, and magical
as a warlock's ancient skin,
branch by branch,
rising toward God
with a breeze tussling the immortality
of our souls.

Near the top, we perched
on a sturdy limb
like red-tailed hawks,
hidden from the adult world,
protected from our parents
fighting on the porch.

Safety in the Arms of the Magnolia

Rachel and I listened to the world
from our secret spot,
the branches of a Magnolia
rooted in the backyard.
The dirt and mysteries of the family
played out on the patio below us.

We heard our parents tearing into flesh,
gnashing at each other's jugular.
The shouts and cries
of their Saturday night arguments
fused with gospel music on the radio,
loud as hallelujahs.

We watched our parents dancing and grinding.
My dad felt Mom's skirt like a bass player
running his big hands down the upright's wide hips.
Love seemed a hard and rough rhythm
driving the body toward the edge of death.

Secrets caught in the branches
like a hot summer breeze.
Mom said Mrs. Johnson cried
when she clipped her husband's
jeans to the clothesline
because he was an alley cat
every Friday night.

Mom said the preacher man
had been scamming God for years.

That was why he was well-fed,
drove a black Cadillac,
and wore a fedora with a feather.
One evening, Mom drank Wild Turkey
and chatted with a neighbor.
Her voice sounded loose and breezy.

She leaned toward her friend:
Rachel was a mistake.
My husband says that's why
she's the dead roots of our family.

Sis held my hand when I cried.

The Brilliant Days

Rachel and I had our brilliant moments
free from the turmoil and damage of the family.
We danced unburdened and alive,
trying to salvage our innocence.

The brilliant morning,
a young virtuoso playing songbirds,
the trill and warble rising to meet daybreak.

The beautiful morning,
dewdrop fresh, bathing in light,
cleansing the world of our past.

The glamorous morning,
a fashionista clothing the earth
in nature's haute couture.

The talented morning,
a master seamstress cutting sharp shadows
and patterns out of dust and dirt.

***

The afternoon, garbed green
and cloudless blue,
beckons us to spring's festival.
We sit on the bank of a river,
the shadows of beech trees
strain toward the light-spangled water.
There is no yesterday or tomorrow.

We wait, sun-warmed,
listening to the river's silent meditation,
watching the trout break the surface
like moments of enlightenment.

***

Twilight cracks open the sun,
Monet's paintbrush dabs and sweeps
light and color across the still water,
capturing an unrepeatable moment.

A solitary fisherman's flatbottom boat
drifts toward the golden hour.
The angler reels in a trout,
releases the fish into the deep water.
Concentric circles ripple toward the bank,
embrace the swaying cattails.

We rise, leaving our awe
among the rocks and smooth pebbles.
Dusk descends,
the dark patina of a day well spent.

Magic Lanterns

Twilight:
magenta, red, and orange
were the colors of tangled kisses
between day and night.

Twilight:
flashing fireflies,
fragrance of flowers in the garden,
fleeting moments of innocence
unhinged from family secrets and sins.

Sis and I chased the bioluminescent lights
with our laughter ringing like windchimes.
Sis taught me to softly cup
the fireflies in my small hands.
She called the glow a magic lantern.
We gloried in moments of hushed joy
before we gently released the glow
back into twilight.

There were nights I trembled
as Dad's words bruised Sis.
The soft glow of her heart
seemed unbearably vulnerable,
easily crushed and ruined
beyond forgiveness.

My Guardian Angel

Sis was the protective one.
She watched me from the kitchen window
playing imaginary games of football
in the backyard.
She hovered above me, a guardian angel.

The window framed her smile,
red hair, sky blue eyes.
Her adoration healed my loneliness.
Her transcendent presence above me
transfigured the dull, cloudy afternoon
into stained-glass light.

When I ran inside,
she knelt in front of me,
wiped the dirt off my blue jeans,
and whispered a blessing:
You're my baby brother,
so strong and fast.

Beachcombers

During our winters at the beach,
Rachel and I became
early morning beachcombers.
The wind flapped our windbreakers
and swept stubborn sorrows and pain
down the beach and into white dunes.

We walked miles of shoreline.
Sand and hope stuck between our toes.
Time expanded endlessly along the horizon,
a canvas stretched on the frame of eternity.

Gray gulls hovered over whitecaps,
plunged for fish,
arced away on hidden wind currents
into a mystical cloak of hazy morning mist.

With our feet slip sliding in the sand,
we collected unbroken shells at low tide,
gathering them in a basket
beside the front door of the cottage,
an offering of bounty and wholeness.

Sis crafted a keepsake necklace
out of rope and the perfect scallop shells.
She studied the handmade necklace
in the mirror, tilted her head, and smiled.
Someday this jewelry will become
the heirloom of my dreams.

500 Miles Away From Home

Every summer, Rachel and I
visited our grandmother's farm
near Aberdeen, North Carolina.

In the evenings, after a shower,
she would wrap her hair in a towel
and sing along to the song "500 Miles"
by Peter, Paul and Mary.

The song was her anthem,
her dream of escape to freedom
from the prison of her family.

She sang the song proud and loud,
and yet, her urgency made me sad.
She felt distant and alone,
like that train whistle blowing in the distance.
She taught me the loneliness of freedom.

At night, safe on the porch,
hiding in shadows and silhouettes,
Sis confided terrible secrets.

I will always feel abandoned
by Dad and a Father God.
Anger clamps down on me,
a hunter's trap biting to bone.
I flee, dragging steel behind me.

Lights glowed in the window
of a red farmhouse in the distance,
the unblinking eyes of a distant God.

That harsh uncompromising truth
breaks my life into small defeats,
small pieces of Eucharist bread.
I taste suffering on my tongue.

The day's humidity and heat
stagnated in the branches
of Magnolia trees.

On these humid, heavy summer nights,
my thoughts hang motionless
in my mind. Today at the creek,
a breeze quivered in aspen trees,
the leaves trembled
like the hands of a dying man.

Day or night, there was no relief
from the heat. The sun burned
the grass brown and dried up the creek.
At night, the drapes billowed and fell,
the heaving chest of God.

Will I always see the world
through the lens of Ash Wednesday?

I fear I'm being dragged
behind the wake of a silent scream.
Our days are oppressive, monotonous
like dying fish strung together
by a rope threaded through the gills.

The whistle blew as the freight train
rambled through town, right on time.
Sis hummed "500 Miles."

There are evenings
I'm already on the train, Baby Brother.
The evenings I hold my smile
in place at the dinner table
like a death mask.
The smile freezes on my face
until I don't know
who I am, where I am.
I board the train to survive,
to redefine myself
as silent loneliness.

We waited for a distant whistle to blow.
I imagined Sis riding away from home,
her frozen smile gradually thawing
into a soft and gentle solitude.

When I'm gone, listen for the whistle,
Baby Brother, and you'll know
I'm far away from home.

Rainstorm on a Lake

Walking a lake in March with my sister,
the trees sway and lean forward
to reflect in the water,
to greet our solitude.

The silence between us
is disfigured and disturbed
by the bellowing of Dad's
morning tirade.

Dragonflies dart colors
against the dark shallows,
fleeting as unspoken fears.

Storm clouds appear in the distance,
ominous, oppressive.
Suddenly, shafts of silver rain
lance the far side of the lake.
The column approaches relentlessly,
carrying unavoidable answers
to questions we refuse to ask.

The movement of the silver rain
is biblical, like the first creation,
like the Spirit of God moving
across the primordial water.

And then it reaches us.
The deluge drenches us
with God's power,
weaves us into creation.

God calls us good in his sight.
The trees and our hearts
tremble with awe.
We laugh, startled and astonished.

The rain moves past us.
We walk toward the bank,
stepping through mud
and over slippery rocks,
feet planted on a new earth.

Slowly, we rest in quiet contentment.
The silence between us transforms
into a perfect grace note.

Our eyes shine like candles in a sacred church.
We realize the simple act
of lighting a candle is a prayer.
The flicker of the candle is hope.

The Scapegoat

Before Rachel left for college,
we huddled together in the secret hideout
on the bank of the river.

She confessed her fears
under the witness of a full moon.
I didn't have ears to hear
the foreshadowing of her death.

Her eyes were clear and sane,
but at the same time
she was somewhere else,
so far away.

She feared college
would be a wilderness experience.
She explained that God
has many reasons for driving
a person into the wilderness.

I dreaded her words.
All I could do was listen
to the water murmuring over stones.

She said God drove Moses
into the wilderness
to prepare him to be a stuttering prophet,
to set his people free,
to lead them through a second wilderness
to the edge of the promised land.

God drove Nebuchadnezzar
into the wilderness of madness
to chastise and humble a king.

God banished Hagar
into the wilderness of despair
to dig a well for her
and create a new nation.

God sent Jesus
into the wilderness
to be tempted by the devil,
to clarify the son of man's purpose.

On the bank of that river,
Sis looked far away and whispered:
Why did God and Dad make me
a scapegoat? They drive me into the wilderness
as a sacrifice for the sins of our family.

My whole life I have tried to rebel
against that role.
Out of fear, I have lived
five hundred miles away from home.
All I know is anger and fear.
I don't know who I am.

We listened to the water
murmuring over stones.

For the first time,
I watched Sis cry.

Promise me, Baby Brother,
don't let me die in the wilderness
and come to me
if you hear that whistle blow.

Suddenly, Rachel's face paled,
she stared at approaching storm clouds
being torn apart by the wind,
her voice lost its soft vulnerability,
and her heart seemed to turn to stone.
She clutched my hand.
If the time comes, Baby Brother,
accept the sacrifice.
Make your life count.

Snow Falling Soft as Grace

After Rachel left for college,
Mom sat on the covered porch
knitting a blanket to send to her.

Snowflakes drifted, beginning to stick
like a memory on the Magnolia branches.
Mom paused and contemplated the snowfall.

Your grandmother used to say
the angels are knitting
a white blanket of snow today.

An unusual sadness bordering
on a resigned grief softened Mom's voice.
She stood and held out her hand
beyond the roof of the porch.
White brushed across her pale skin,
melted on her palm.

Mom sat back down, placed her needles
and yarn on the porch table, and took my hand.
Gone was her usual lowered-gaze meekness.
She blessed me with the fierce eye contact
of compassion and honesty.
She took a deep breath and exhaled,
finally resolved to say what needed to be said.

There are no warm blankets for Rachel.
Your father stole her innocence.

I squeezed Mom's frigid hand.
Don't say that.
I want her to be happy at Carnegie Mellon
and visit on vacation.

Mom stared at the light snowfall
beginning to cover the front yard.
I wish I could cry tears of snow for her.
No one will ever see her paintings.

Mom kissed my hand
and pressed it against her cheek.
Is she a missing part of you, Mom?

Mom covered her face,
her hands trembled, her shoulders shook
as she wept tearless tears.
All these years, I never stopped him.

Mom looked at me with a great sadness.
I could see the tears behind her eyes.
I wanted her to cry.
Sis said some suffering
can only be seen through tears.

Mom whispered:
It's hard to bear the white snow
today that's falling soft as grace.

Almost Redeemed

My father lay on the hospital bed,
his hardened heart failing.
Old Testament judgment no longer roared
from dark flashing eyes.

He trembled, a shell of the patriarch
who ruled the family with an iron fist.
Sis, the one he bruised and slaughtered,
refused to visit him.
I won't play the scapegoat again
and carry his shame and sin
into another wilderness.

My father clung to life,
he wrestled with unfinished business.
He patted a photograph of Rachel
that rested on his heaving chest.
With a raspy voice muffled
by his oxygen mask, he asked me
to write a letter to her.

My ballpoint pressed down on blank paper,
scratching out unholy words:
My girl, honey, please.

He closed his eyes and knocked
the mask off his face,
struggling for simple words:
Remember, you sat on my knee,
you said you were riding a horse
into the sunset.

My father gripped the sheets.
He didn't know how to cry.
I urged him to finish his plea.
Now I'm riding into the sunset
where I can never wound you again.

Then he lay in the quiet brutality of silence,
almost redeemed by what he tried to say.

His only mistake: he survived.
His leather lungs returned.
The three-way bypass
failed to change his heart.

Letters From Carnegie Mellon

Sis danced toward the edges
of oblivion, trying to find safety
and freedom in distance from home.
But she knew the swelter
of living in Dad's presence.
She knew one day the songs would end.

She escaped to Carnegie Mellon
on an art scholarship.
She rarely saw Dad again,
but the memories tracked
the scent of her fears.

Sis sent me short letters
from Carnegie Mellon during the first year.
She seemed strong,
swimming against the current of her childhood.
Her teachers praised her,
said her paintings fractured eye sockets.

She lived unfettered and alive
without flinching at loud sounds
or watching for danger
lurking in her peripheral vision.

She had a boyfriend and thrived
on the "mystery and mirage"
of young love.

One afternoon, they tipped
their canoe on a lake.

Sis splashed her boyfriend
in the face as she surfaced.
They kissed in the shelter
of the overturned canoe.
He tasted dangerous,
like a broken curfew.

That night in their dorm,
they slept under sheet lightning
blanketing the sky.

In the morning, she sketched a self-portrait:
an unrestrained canvas of memories
and a palette knife of loneliness
layered her impasto beautiful.
She felt dangerous, like love.

Gradually, her letters darkened.
She broke up with her boyfriend.
The pain felt like shrapnel
lodged too close to her heart.

She spiraled downward like Icarus
with broken and burning wings.
She had flown too close to the sun.

The letters never lied.
Her strength began to unravel.
Her thoughts were swept away
from safety and shore
by a riptide of depression and despair.

I was trapped at home.
My love couldn't reach her,
the undercurrent refused to release her.
I could feel the current running
hard and fast underneath the silence.
My best friend was drowning before my eyes.

The letters and the music she loved
disintegrated into silence.
But I knew Sis.
I knew she would keep on dancing
to the gypsy ballads dying in her mind,
and the beauty of her desperate dancing
made her my hero.

Blind Willie's Jazz Club

I visited Rachel after she dropped out of school.
For a week, she took me to Blind Willie's Club
to listen to a friend sing.

Sis and her friend both saw the world
through embers glowing in their eyes,
the embers and ashes
of their burned down histories.

Sis had started painting again.
She lived a starving artist's life,
painting pictures with the ferocious heat
of a blast furnace.

During the day, the friend worked
the day shift in the factory,
drinking black coffee from a thermos
and listening to Loretta Lynn
on the radio during breaks.

At night,
the singer owned the dive bar.
Nothing scared her,
she'd seen her share of shattered
beer bottles and pool cues,
fights that left men spitting blood,
scars on faces rough as rawhide.

She was a plain-faced girl from Texas,
wearing tight jeans, leather boots,
a bandanna bleeding red.

Her voice had the coarse grit
of a belt sander
sanding down dreams,
leaving sawdust in the air.

She strangled the microphone
like a serial killer
who could bring men
to their knees,
begging for a second chance.

Her songs were primordial,
mouth warped and wailing
like giving birth to the first child
marked with sin.

She sang to the sweltering heat
of a Lone Star summer.

Night after night
she showed the crowd
what it was like to improvise,
to die a loud and hard death.

After last call,
the three of us
leaned against her car,
watching and listening
to trucks grinding gravel
in the parking lot.

The friend wanted her voice
to crush the stars and blind the moon.
She dreamed
of clocking out of nine-to-five routines
and the dead-end escape of strong whiskey.

They both needed to discover
something that put them on edge,
made their hearts skip a beat with fear
or love or the unknown.

Sis told me the friend left one day
without a word, a note, or a song.
Sis escaped her life years later.
I never heard the whistle blow.

The View From a Balcony

My sister is down and out.
She slouches on a balcony
with curlers in her hair,
dragging on a cigarette.

A black metal fire escape
climbs a wall in an alley
toward the balcony,
rising like Jacob's ladder
into outer darkness.
Her genius has rotted into madness,
voodoo chants lurk behind her eyes.

She drinks Wild Turkey on the rocks,
scanning the streets
for the silhouette of her cheating man.

Below her, car lights scrape over ice.
The moon throws silver light
onto snow-covered asphalt

A man in a full-length winter coat
disappears into neon lights
where dancers whisper
with gold dust in their voices
and hope distills
to shots of cheap whiskey.

Bowed streetlights line the avenue,
burdened with snow
like bent tree branches.

A homeless man
buries his head in his hands,
swipes at the falling snow,
trudges into an alley
like a crippled animal.

Across the street in a flop house,
lights seethe in windows,
a saxophone on a radio
screams like a patient in a madhouse.

My sister flicks
the stub of her cigarette
over the balcony
like a burnt-out dream,
finishes her drink,
watches the moon
go blind and mad behind clouds.

The Wailing Wall

After hitting rock bottom,
Rachel careened from psych hospitals
to addiction treatment programs.

She was manic and psychotic,
speaking in tongues,
talking dirty to the gods.
Her exquisite metaphors
turned florid and flamboyant.

She crashed and burned
and grieved her smoldering wings.
She shuffled mindlessly
from empty hour to empty hour,
dragging from shadow to shadow,
her thoughts soggy and limp.

She self-medicated
with whiskey and beer, passed out,
groping for a comfortable numbness.
Her thoughts were stale,
like the crushed cigarette butts
overflowing her ashtrays.

I visited her in the hospital
and found her standing
in front of a white wall
in the hallway, frozen
before her personal Wailing Wall.

I led her to the garden,
and she insisted on sharing
the prayers she would slip
into a crack in the wall.

Deep in thought, she stared
at a cluster of rose bushes
and lit a Camel cigarette.

*Once I told you prayer
was rebellion against despair.
Now prayer is desperation
to connect with something
greater than myself.*

Her cigarette hissed in a plastic cup.

*First, I want off my medications.
They bloat my face and my thoughts.
They inflict a death before death.*

Sis lit another cigarette.

*I want God to heal my sight,
to release the tears
trapped behind my eyes.*

She paused and blew a smoke ring.

Maybe all I truly want is to believe enough
to really pray. Remember the women
in the cathedral we used to visit?

I closed my eyes, pictured
the old women in kerchiefs scattered
in the wooden pews like worn hymnals,
heads bowed before the altar of a dying God,
muttering prayers in foreign languages.

I nodded as Sis whispered:
That's how I want to pray,
like I believe God.
I'm a bruised and bent reed,
and he has promised not to break me.

Family Therapy

The therapist clarified:
Rachel is searching
for her lost identity.

That awful evening
before Sis left for college
roared in my mind:
the broken-down confession,
the restraints of anger and fear,
the unraveling rebellion
against the scapegoat role.

Sis smirked.
I'm searching for my lost identity
at the bottom of an empty shot glass,
sifting through myths, stories,
delusions, and flamboyant lies.

The therapist leaned forward
toward Sis.
And what have you found?

I am more than
my medical records, she blurted out.
As a teenager at the beach,
I flew a blue diamond kite,
pretending it was my soul,
free, unfeeling, and untouchable,
hovering above the pain,
dipping to almost skim the waves
and rising to merge with the twilight.

I silently burned in an unquenchable
sadness, trying to conjure
faded and blurred images of that evening.
I couldn't remember the shape of the kite,
the color of my mother's swimsuit,
the beauty of the sunset,
the rare and awkward smile of my father,
the brilliant fireworks in my sister's
sky blue eyes flaring like the twilight.

Sis continued to rant:
I can't be cured by positive thoughts.
As an adult, I walk the beach,
and my shadow stains the white sand.

Sis clapped her hands.

My traumas and sins are written
on my soul with indelible ink.
Sis paused.
I take that back. They are written
on my soul with invisible ink.

Sis turned directly toward me:
I now embrace the darkness,
knowing it envelops the light.
You will never know me,
Baby Brother, until you touch
the fearful delusions.

The therapist glanced at me,
questioning—*You look troubled.*

I shrugged and squeezed my hands together,
trying to grind down my thoughts to the pain.
I've been touched
by either God or death.
I can't tell the difference.

Years later, after Sis was gone,
I realized what I had wanted to say
to the therapist:
When the magenta
of twilight embraced my sister,
I knew God had created her for eternity.

The Heirloom of Her Dreams

Rachel is back in the hospital.
We sit across from each other
at a wooden table in the hospital's garden.
She stares at me with vacant eyes—
mottled windows into her hollow soul.
My heart pounds in my chest—
echoes reverberating in a carved-out canyon.

Her hair, red like Mom's, is gone.
Sis shaved it off the night
the paramedics found her.
I want to save her.
Our shadows almost touch.

Sis condemns our mom
for abandoning her.
There is no excuse for Mom's failure
to intervene, for the cover-up with make-up
and long-sleeved shirts in summer.

I try to view Mom with grace.
I was there after you left
for Carnegie Mellon.
Mom grieved her failure
to protect you.

Sis slams her fist on the table.
A little late!

I try to walk in Mom's shoes.
Mom was scared to leave.
She grew up dirt poor

and her family lost their farm
during the Depression.
Can't you see,
she wanted to protect you,
but she was fighting the wrath of God.
She was trapped just like us.

The wind begins to sweep away
the lingering afternoon heat in the garden.

Don't minimize Mom's failures
or my suffering, Baby Brother.
You can't see past the adoration
between you two.
You were like the Madonna and Christ Child
trapped in stained glass.
You've never been able to break free
from that glass.

Stunned by the vicious truth,
I sit back and treat my open wounds.
Maybe Sis was right.

Questions without answers strangle our words,
forgiveness withers in the lingering heat.
Silence beats on us hard as our father's fist.

Slowly, the day cracks open
into delusions of color.
My sister's lips quiver.

How many times had I seen that look
as fear and pain
backwashed into her heart.

I've waited for this chance
to reclaim Sis,
but in her shattered presence,
the desire seems torn and frayed at the edges.
I reach for her hand. She pulls away,
but she can't deny our history.

Sis takes a long inhale.
Look at the clouds closing over
the emerging stars like cataracts of grief.
Neither of us can see the truth.

Dusk obliterates color.
Rachel's silhouette merges with darkness.
Visiting hours are over.
We stand to go back to her room.

I clench my teeth,
torn apart by a moon
halved into darkness and light.
I am lost. I fumble for grace.
Can I visit tomorrow?

The shadow of Sis whispers:
I'd like that.
Maybe you can bring me
the unbroken shells,
the heirloom of my dreams.

Someone I Love Is Going Insane

Someone I love is going insane,
hurtling towards another attempt
to leave this world,
desperate to terminate the pain.

Over the phone, Sis admitted
she hated the snow falling
in sheets of purity
against the backdrop of darkness.

She despised the snowplows
grinding through time,
leaving behind the salt
of the earth and black ice.

She confessed she was painting again,
as if creativity was a weakness
and colors were an unwanted affirmation of hope.

She was painting a self-portrait,
tracing the traumas of her life
carved like razor slices
on her pale and gaunt face.

The electricity in her house
had been shut off,
but she insisted she was dancing
to the flickering mystery of candles.

That call is the reason
I'm in my car,

the heat blasting,
trying to thaw my fear
into the courage of a savior.

When we were young,
didn't we laugh together,
making an ugly world right again?
Sometimes I slept on her floor
on a rug beside her bed.

We listened to our father
in the next room,
fortifying his cruelty with liquor.
I pretended Sis was my guardian angel.

That call is the reason
I'm driving towards her house
past streetlamps haloed
with light in the falling snow.

I promised to save her from the wilderness,
to listen for the train whistle blowing.
My prayer is that she still has a thirst to live.

I look around.
Her darkness touches me.
Everything seems as hideous
as her rundown and broken mind.

A black car slides on ice.
Another is abandoned
on the side of the road.

Dark and closed bars
and restaurants line the road.
The piles of snow pushed
against the sidewalk by plows
are already dirty with the grime of exhaust.

For months I've abandoned her,
fallen asleep while she cried
tears of blood in her private Gethsemane.
Now I grip the steering wheel,
demanding God to relent
and remove this cross from her future.

I've moved from room to room
in my small house,
comfortable and numb in my forgetfulness.
The days have been ordinary.
I've eaten a bowl of soup
or sipped a glass of wine
without imagining the insanity
growing inside Sis like a tumor.

Sis didn't even intrude into my memory.
There was a time our fantasies and lore
fought off her madness.
Am I now running to rescue her
or fleeing the memories
that condemn me?

I park in front of her ranch-style house.
No interior lights are on.

The house is a frozen carcass
rotting in outer darkness.

Doom strangles me. I feel the magnetic
pull of psychosis.
I exhale vapor and stumble over roots
in the yard shrouded by a layer of snow.

Weeds grasp at shinbones.
I pull my winter coat tight,
knock on the door.
She refuses to open it,
calling me the incarnation of our father.
I wrestle with that ghost guarding the entrance.

Friend or foe? Rachel shouts.

I can't speak the language
of the insane or the dying.
Friend, I stutter.

That's not good enough, she demands.

Your brother.

She dismisses my answer.
Not good enough.

Baby Brother, I desperately guess.

Ah. Come in, Baby Brother.
It's been a while.

A Brilliant Madness

When I entered my sister's house
that night, Rachel was no longer Sis.

Madness sparked in her eyes
and then went dark,
a power outage of her soul.

Her hand trembled
as she strangled the neck
of a whiskey bottle.

Her voice crashed against me
like surging high tide waves
and suddenly hushed to the stillness
of a windless low tide.

She spoke in tongues to manic gods,
cramming a billion universes into a word,
explaining the quantum physics of miracles,
burning the ordinary to ashes with Pentecostal flames.

Out of work, no electricity,
she perched, enchanted,
on the edge of the couch,
listening in silent awe to angels
chanting on an unplugged radio.

Her mind darted like a hummingbird
from one loose association to the next,
searching for the nectar
of grandiosity and transcendence.

She lit five candles
that glowed like the eyes of bold ghosts
and performed a séance with the dead in the dark.

She slashed her collection of paintings
with a knife as a sacrificial offering to the Devil
and chain-smoked on the edge of chaos,
burning her cigarettes into the soft skin of darkness.

Her words jostled and shoved me off-balance.
I bled with empathy for her,
but fear clotted on my vocal cords.

I tried to whisper to Sis buried below
the tombstones in her eyes,
tried to woo her into treatment with memories,
but she carved at my words with her cigarette,
scratched at my face to find Dad
hiding below the skin.

She threatened me with delusions,
demanding that I renounce the request,
claiming she was a red-haired Gorgon
like Mom and would turn me into stone.

The thought of treatment agitated her.
She prowled into the kitchen
like a caged tigress
and shouted as if she had discovered
a revelation, *Fuck you. You better run.*

She exploded out of the kitchen, waving
a butcher knife. *You better run.*
Time couldn't contain the intensity of the moment,
and fear tore apart the seams of poetry.

Savage thoughts and words hurtled toward
a head-on collision with trauma.
I scrambled to my feet but walked slowly
toward the front door to avoid
any sudden movements.

The sacrificial lamb had turned violent,
bent on slitting the throat of a high priest,
intent on replacing forgiveness with revenge.
She wanted to rewrite the sacred.

I opened the front door and stepped outside,
but I kept the door cracked enough to see
and talk to her. My hope had narrowed to a crack
in Rachel's wooden door. I couldn't lose her.
I begged for her to go with me to treatment.

Rachel stormed to the door
and tried to shove it closed. I resisted.
We hit a stalemate. Our straining faces
were a foot apart as we pushed against each other.
Suddenly, her face softened, and her eyes bloomed
like morning glory in morning light.
Sis, not Rachel, whispered to me
from a precious childhood memory,
Wow, Baby Brother. You're so strong.

Her transformation to Sis drained my strength.
I stepped back and let my arms drop by my side.
Rachel or Sis, it no longer mattered, closed the door.
The deadbolt clicked shut.

I jogged around to the front windows.
Rachel danced around the room,
surrounded by glowing candles,
swaying her hands above her head.
I wondered if the angels were singing
glory hallelujah on the unplugged radio.

Her celebration at my expense
incinerated my compassion.
She wasn't my sister anymore.
I felt contaminated by her delusions.
A strange cruelty overtook me.

I picked up a handful of pebbles
and raked them across the front windows.
Rachel fell to the floor like she'd been shot
and crawled on her belly to hide behind a desk.

Every few minutes, she poked her head up
to look at the windows and then withdrew
again behind the desk. I watched
from the distance of an emotionless god.

Enough was enough.
The snow started to pour down
without mercy.

The wind sounded like vespers
whispered by angels.
I refused to weep.
Everything ends,
even pain, even sorrow.
I trudged to my car
and silently headed home.

I left Sis afraid, doomed, damned.

The Call

The call: my sister was gone.
I walked the winter streets,
alone and abandoned by Sis.
The unfathomable call jolted
and shifted the axis of the earth.

Storm clouds draped
the moon in a dark shroud.
My heart collapsed into silence,
a silence that felt like I was trapped
in the empty space behind a falling star.

The grief was personal and intimate.
The pain came to me
whispering in my sister's voice,
calling me by my given name,
changing my breathing
with frayed images of our childhood.

When I arrived at my sister's house,
her body had been wheeled away,
but I found her tormented soul
in her paintings stored in the attic.

Brushstroke by brushstroke,
her loneliness and mental illness
created self-portraits that were part
paint, part desperation.

Her life seemed like dried paint
on a palette, like beautiful colors
that never transformed
into the mystery of a painting.

I wept, realizing she couldn't paint
her way back to sanity.
With a brush, or a pen, or a dream
she couldn't paint herself
back to a fragile humanity
or find a vulnerable truce
with her despair.

The Empty Bottle on My Sister's Nightstand

I try to make sense
of the empty bottle
on my sister's nightstand.
The obvious seems too obvious.
Dad's fist left bruises
that turned purple like the cloth
draped over the cross during Lent.
She never cried
at the meaningless sacrifice.

She staggered through hidden
stations of the cross, waiting
for the stillness at the end
of a crucifixion that offered
no forgiveness,
resurrection, or redemption.

Her moods swung like a pendulum.
She brooded, painting shattered
self-portraits I couldn't repair.
She danced the night away,
arms raised, eyes closed, encircled
by nameless northern boys from Harvard.

I visited her after she lost her job.
Her hatred for Dad was growing
inside her, malignant.
Alcohol couldn't blunt the pain.

Last time I saw her,
anger, grief, and despair
fought and struggled like netted fish
inside her chest.

I wonder, in the end,
trapped in her delusions,
did she mean to cut the net?
Did the strands burst,
releasing her suffering
back into the deepest depths
of a clear blue lake?

Eulogy in the Cathedral

The eulogy of my father
echoed in the empty cathedral,
a blasphemy against Rachel's life.

He lied. Before the ceremony,
he called her suicide self-slaughter,
a shameful and selfish act,
but he covered up the sin.
He changed the cause of death
on the death certificate to a heart attack.

In the eulogy, he praised her love of nature,
her careful tending of her garden.
He left out her painting, the bruises, the rebellion,
the tragic spiral into mental illness and addiction.
We sang hymns and listened to Bible verses.

In the end, it didn't matter, no one
was there to listen or weep.

The real eulogy was the empty pews
and the silence of God's love.
I sat in the front row, staring
at the massive organ pipes
hovering over us
like the naked ribs of a Savior,
quiet and breathless.

Eulogies in Blind Willie's Jazz Club

I visited Blind Willie's Club,
Rachel's favorite jazz bar,
after her death.
I pieced together eulogies
from fragments of conversations
with strangers and Rachel's friends.

***

We met on a school trip
to Paris before she left Carnegie Mellon.
We studied the Impressionists.

In Paris, we fell in love with a fantasy,
enchanted by the lost generation,
the bohemian lifestyle,
the café culture,
the freedom to improvise joy
and carefree nights.

In the sleepless city of light,
we danced scandalously,
buoyed by champagne
and illusions of the Belle Epoque.
We fancied ourselves
breaking the rules, immortalized
in lithographs drawn by Toulouse Lautrec.

We carried the reverie back home
like souvenirs to the city that never sleeps.

Our dreams remained larger than life,
like advertisements in Time Square.

She pulled off heroin chic
and I wore black skinny ties.

After a few years, we lost our way.
I was enslaved to billable hours.
She painted the growing
darkness of her soul.

At night, we slept
with our backs to each other.
Our hands blurred over our bodies.
We lost the intimacy of touch.
But the old French songs died hard.
They lingered on the life support of memories.
Surely, we would wake up in Paris again.

In the end, I simply learned the art of atrophy
and preserved my heart on ice.
I still don't know if my leaving
betrayed her or whether I was saving myself.

Today, I remember Paris,
wondering whether salvation still quivers
from a jazz quartet in Duc des Lombards?

Wouldn't it be grand
if we could have swept away the years.

In Montparnasse, we would dance away
our nightmares and broken hearts
and toast with champagne
fresh and sultry dreams.

I would smile like the crescent moon
as we improvise joy again
and Rachel dances a savage Charleston
stolen from Josephine Baker.

*****

I remember an exhibition
of her paintings:
a single leaf torn from a branch,
drifting downriver;
driving snow and blinding mist
devouring color;
the angry cigarette of a silhouette
scarring the darkness;
a scared and desperate teenager
in punk-rocker black
slouching against a wall in a bus terminal.

She even sold one painting
of an old six-story brick apartment building.
Empty windows shone with light at night
except for a single window
framing a solitary shadow.
The dark figure was inaccessible,
nameless, faceless, motionless.

I didn't have eyes to see
the isolation, the painful
and darkening beauty
of her growing displacement and distance.

*****

Last time I saw Rachel,
her pain was deep, so damn deep,
almost too deep to look at,
like that long-ago cry of desolation.

As I witnessed her agony,
I grew more human and flawed.

***

I called out to her as she walked away.
She didn't answer.
I watched her put her head down
and plow into the winter storm,
knowing her tattered days
would turn monochromatic gray.

A sadness overtook me.
I was watching in real-time
the bottom fall out of her dreams.

I remembered the nights we defied storms,
walking arm-in-arm, dream and dream
back to our apartment after a concert,
with the lingering sound of a saxophone
howling our passions and dreams
at the full moon.

The Eulogy of a Counterculture Friend

I have cancer.
As I face my death,
there is a serenity in living
past the dreams and despair.

The dwindling of time
sifts the ordinary from the sacred.
In my sickness, I glimpse eternity
through the ashes of grief.

A week ago, I learned of your sister's death.
Her heart was the fluttering
of a psychedelic-colored hummingbird.

This morning, I walked our path
through Rock Creek Park with a cane,
honoring her with memories.

As you know, out of the chaos
of her childhood,
she created and owned her spiritual space,
a lone wolf surviving on a tundra,
rewilded and unfettered.

Alone and solitary, she whirled and spun,
uninhibited and carefree
like the kiss of the untamable wind.

I discarded the useless burdens
of the past along the path.
I wanted to travel light with her.

I have wasted too many years
mourning the mundane,
rocking in front of funeral pyres,
watching relationships burn
down to charred embers and ashes.

But the images of your sister still contain
the breath of life. She remains
an old soul in my mind,
furiously flaming in the skin and bones
of a teenage body.

Your sister could be magical.
She ladled stardust into my overcast soul.
Her red hair borrowed from Ireland
fell to her hips like a cascading waterfall.
Her whispers freed songs caught for centuries
in the throat of a god.

When she flew away,
she carried the living heartbeat
of the 60s with her.
For a while, I believed
she would appear at my door,
a pure dove returning with an olive branch
of peace with God,
returning to solid ground after the flood.

As the 60s faded and washed away,
I realized we could never go back
to the innocence.

A friend told me disillusionment
had clamped onto her.

I wept for the end of innocence,
imagining her gnawing off a limb
to escape a trap, to survive,
to keep on suffering for another day.

I knew her pain, so many passion plays,
so many needless deaths on the nightly news,
so many crosses to carry.

Like me, she must have dulled the pain
and drudgery,
finding dark spaces to keep her comfortably numb.
I was afraid to call her, to hear the lament
of a disintegrating goddess turning mortal.

When I heard she had died,
my grief was the gnashing of teeth.
I wanted to wash her body with denial,
to resurrect her into the past.

I tried to dream her into the best years
when she smoked reefer in a coffee house,
eyes closed, her spiritual vision wide open,
enchanted with the protest poetry of Dylan.
Her style was boho before it became chic,
an improvised riot of color,
a flow of handmade paradise.

I thought the best I could do now is drag
my grief and pain from loneliness to loneliness.
I believed the stark reality of my looming death
had mellowed my grief into contentment.
But your sister's death
has taught me to weep again.

I heard the news while seated
in my oncologist's waiting room,
surrounded by fellow chemo patients.
I realized she had taught me everything
I needed to know:
I am a human being: alive, beautiful, and dying.

Grieving During the First Year

That first summer after Rachel's death,
I rotted on the porch, watching
the sprinklers arch over burnt grass.

I lay in rigor mortis on the blue loveseat
in the blue-walled study,
feeling only the odd tilt of the earth's axis,
wishing my wife would close the blinds
before my eyes burned the noonday sun.

Each day the sky darkened to dusk.
The silhouette of a willow
bowed to the ground,
a penitent clothed in black.

When I visited the river,
large branches floated with the current,
carrying my silent pleas for healing.

I couldn't clean out
her bohemian skirts from her closet,
or empty her drawers
filled with diamond earrings
and gold bracelets
that jangled when she danced,
healthy and vibrant
in Blind Willie's Jazz Club.

Winter came with a fury.
The emaciated branches
were gray and brown,
the color of dust and dirt.

The skeleton trees begged for relief,
pleading for buds and bloom.
They were the images of degradation,
sackcloth, and numb prayers,
the unbearable ache for an unreachable spring.

I Am Undone

Grief has no narrative arc.
It lacks the truth of time and coherence.
It creates an illusion, splicing together loosely
associated memories and emotions
across time,
leaving half of Rachel's life
on the cutting room floor.

Grief merges my existence
into her pain.
I have become an extension
of her suffering.
I am the resurrection
of her agony.

I commit a slow suicide with whiskey.
I dilute the unbearable images
into sacred symbols and distant dreams.

I am undone.
I have become my father.
I have become my sister.
I have become my God.

The Gas Station

Driving home from a bar
late at night, enflamed with whiskey.
Someone needs to pay
for the martyrdom of my sister.

In my mind, I'm a terrorist
creating Molotov cocktails
out of dangerous thoughts.
I want to burn shit down.

I've missed my meds for a week.
I'm strangling the steering wheel
like my father about to lose it
on our long family car rides
to the New Jersey shore.

I understand him now that I spiral
toward sporadic eruptions.
I need quiet from the grating
gears of a repetitive world.

When I rant, I startle even
an all-knowing God.
My anger sets flame
to the best parts of me.
Forgiveness, grace, and compassion
are simply kindling wood
for my rage.

I stop at the Chevron
and spear my old Honda
with the gas nozzle.

Above me, the moon
is a white dinner plate
broken in half.
The world seems cracked,
shattered.
My heart withdraws
into silence.

The cars on the street
pass by the station
without sound.
Unheard, unstoppable seconds
force me toward death
like a moving walkway
in a crowded airport.

I am detached and distant
from my life.
My sins and compassion,
my love and hatred,
my belief and disbelief
are mirages.

Nothing matters, nothing is mine.
I am alone, utterly alone
in a godless world.

There is a strange peace below
the surface turmoil of meaninglessness.

In this timeless moment, I finally grasp
the pain below my anger.

The grief feels like a wet rope
sliding through my grip,
stripping flesh, leaving rope burns.

Then, just as suddenly, sound returns:
the swish of cars on the street,
the chatter of the attendant,
the Billy Joel song seeping
out of the Honda's
half-cracked window.

The gears begin to grind again.
I slip into the driver's seat
and call my wife,
reassuring her I'm headed home.

I turn up the radio
and sing along
as I grip the steering wheel
and hold on for dear life.

A Deer Drinks From White Water

I want to write my way out of this cemetery
with oak trees lining the path to my sister's grave.
I want to write my way to the river
where we listened to white water sing over rocks.

I want to eat the same lunch we did that day—
peanut butter and honey sandwiches
and tea poured from a thermos.
I want the trees to protect us
with shadows etched and patterned by God.

I want to smile at my sister's hope
as it curves and arcs like a long fly cast
into a future at Carnegie Mellon.
I want to listen to her voice
sing like those smooth river rocks.
I want to sit on the hard cold dirt on the hill
and watch Sis sleep on a brown blanket,
feeling safe enough to close her eyes.

I want to write my way there
to ask the water
if it remembers sweeping away
the girl's lost dreams, the ones
that turned out to be as light
and insubstantial as autumn leaves
tumbling down the river.

I want to ask if the river remembers
the deer that came out of the trees
to drink the white water.

I want to remember what I felt
as Sis slept, and I gazed
at the delicate mouth of the deer
drinking from the swirling current.

I want to write my way back to the sun
that caressed my sister's face
and gently awaken her
from her frayed innocence.
I want her to drink for a beautiful moment
from the white water as it sings to a deer.

A Letter to My Sister Safe in Heaven

Dear Shaman, Weaver of Myths, Slayer of Enemies.

Time to turn away from your suicide
and remember our secret hiding place
on the bank of a river that flowed
through the woods behind our house.

We sat on the bank. Your words,
wrapped and hushed in secrets and mysteries,
felt like the cool water
embracing our bare feet and ankles.

We rested in the shade of aspen trees.
You named the shadows God's calligraphy
and whispered the comforting messages
patterned on dirt, water, and cattails.

You seemed wise and transcendent
as light and dark played on your perfect face
and you weaved worlds without Dad's fists
or Mom's cold stained glass beauty.

You created myths: the gentle wind
brushing our faces and stirring leaves
came from the beating of angel wings
as the guardians hovered protectively above us.

The rush of water leaping over rocks
was the gleeful and mischievous sound
of ancient gods and martyrs laughing
in a paradise emptied of despair.

We skipped rocks, embedding them
on the opposite bank, pretending
the stones were thudding into the forehead
of a Goliath shaped like our father.

We whooped and hollered, never tiring
of the repeated slaughter and victory
over our fiercest and greatest enemy.
We danced and sang songs of celebration.

Dear Hero of the Resistance, Leader of the Rebellion,
Scapegoat Driven Into the Wilderness.

Our home was enemy territory ruled
by our abusive father
who embodied the wrath of God.

In your teenage years, you grew bold
in your rebellion and resistance,
dancing down and dirty in the basement

to Bruce Springsteen, smoking cigarettes
stolen from Dad, laughing as you guzzled
a six-pack of Budweiser.

I watched in awe and fear at your high-wire act
on the edge of death. You were a live wire
dancing in the street after a storm.

When you left for college, our father
disowned you, banished his scapegoat
to a rocky and inhospitable wilderness.

The night before you left,
we huddled in our hiding place,
and you lamented your loneliness

as the scapegoat without blemish
driven into the wilderness as a sacrifice
for our family's sins.

You touched my cheek like a shadow
trapped in the dusk and whispered:
Accept the sacrifice, Baby Brother.
Make your life count.

Dear Houdini, Survivor, Painter of Trauma.

Forgive me for refusing to accept
your sacrificial slaughter.
I cheered as I watched
your Volkswagen bug back out
of our driveway for the last time,

believing you were an escape artist
miraculously freeing your life
from the shackles of a childhood hell,
believing you were a survivor
fleeing whole and unbroken into a new life.

You wrote me from college.
You were healing by painting your trauma,
turning suffering into art.

Your voice spiked into the maniacal,
the teachers say my paintings break eye sockets.

Dear Sufferer of Butterfly Madness, Unlit Votive Candles,
Broken Angel Dying of Suicide,
Stain on a Bedroom Floor.

In high school for your school science project,
we netted butterflies in a field
and pinned them to felt in a glass case.

The last time I saw you, your house was a hovel
and your brilliant blue eyes
had changed to unlit votive candles.
You showed me the broken case
empty of butterflies.

I've set them free, you ranted
as your hands swooped, floated,
and quivered through the air.
The beautifully insane symbol
shook me to the core.

A month later, the mailman
smelled your decay through the mail slot.
Your trauma left an empty
pill box on the bedside table,
and your body left a stain on the floor.

I scrubbed and scrubbed at the stain
until my wrists gave out.

My father covered the stain
on the hardwood floor with a rug
and sold the house.

I learned that even guardian angels
die and decay in a brutal world.

Dear Pathway to My Salvation,
Memories Sacred as Worn Amulets,
Nostalgia Fresh as a Spring Rain.

Since your death, I have followed your paths
through the Valley of Death and the Valley of Tears.
My mind has unraveled into madness and addiction.
Your memories are the grace
that got me to the other side of trauma.

I am old. I have settled into serenity.
I keep your memories in my pocket
like sacred and well-worn amulets.
Your broken wings taught me to fly
like a red-tailed hawk kiting
over a field plush with golden wheat
swaying to the winds of our youth.

As I tend my garden, gentle downpours
of nostalgia renew the earth and soil.
I think of you as I watch the flowers bloom.

Sis, I have made my life count.

The Waves Die at My Feet

I stroll the beach alone,
breathing salty air,
scent of childhood vacations
with my sister, grieving
moments of devotion
ephemeral as a breeze
sweeping memories
into the dunes.

God plays the keyboard
of the surf.
I nestle into the quiet
spaces between the chords,
the secret places
of guarded memories.

A gull veers over whitecaps,
transfigures golden
in noon's glare,
remembrance of Rachel's face
blinded by brilliance of light.

I imagine her life force burning
beside me, caught between
sun's sultry stare and white-hot sand.

The tide moves slowly,
the ocean tumbles pebbles
at my feet.

The ebb,
the flow,
embrace my ankles.
I realize Rachel's fate
is no longer tethered to the moon.

The ebb,
the flow,
wet sand sticks
between my toes.

Swells heave and sigh,
the ocean's grieving chest
rises and falls.
I close my eyes,
cherishing a glimpse
of Rachel's silhouette in my mind.

A breeze strokes
my graying hair,
for a moment
I almost dream her soul
back into flesh and blood.

The ocean waves die at my feet.

A Glimmer of Grace

I have lost Sis.
I cease to feel
the grandeur of the world.

I ride a city bus,
seated next to a stranger
with holes in her stockings,
my body crammed
against the dirty window.

I exit at a public park
where Sis and I
used to walk.
Her face was bloated
from too much drinking
and her speech was blunted
from the medication.

She confessed she felt
twisted, writhing in torment,
like the elm trees.
Now, I carry her traumas,
suffocated by bitter sadness
and loneliness. I wonder if
I will ever truly love again.

I watch an old man
walking with a cane,
gasping for air.

I realize life comes
to nothing really, hardly
a moment on earth,
a mere breath, a caesura.

White clouds sweep
across a blue sky
like memories of Sis,
convincing me
I'm capable
of dreaming again.

A Walk in the Cemetery

Mom and I walked the cemetery path
lined with oaks
defying death with deep thick roots,
denying grief with twisted branches
encased in ice.

A snowfall,
soft as unbearable forgiveness,
blanketed my sister's grave,
erasing her forsaken name.
Grace withheld by God bruised her soul
more than Dad's merciless wrath.

Mom turned toward me,
her sad eyes struggling
to find me through the lens
of Alzheimer's:
Listen, son,
your father taught you the feel,
the weight of his leather belt.

She was right, I saw the world
through my sister's ashes.
Our father's will
bent us both towards
self-destruction.

Dusk slowly collapsed
on the horizon,
Mom's statuesque silhouette
bent double under the weight
of motherlove and grief.

She wept,
bracketed my cheeks
with warm wrinkled hands,
whispered, lucid and lyrical
like a dusting of snow:
Listen,
I hear Rachel's voice tonight.

I shook my head, entombed in God's silence.

Listen! She urged.

What does she sound like, Mom?

Grace, a tuning fork
struck upon your heart.

I Dream My Sister Alive and Radiant

The slanting rain lances the roof
at night—the gods weep
for your death.
Will the tears flood the earth?

I lie in bed, longing to sleep,
to dream you alive, radiant,
aged peacefully beyond
the year of your suicide.

Perhaps we'll sit in a café,
sipping coffee and eating croissants,
and you'll tell me
you've chosen life over death.

Perhaps we'll walk the arboretum.
You'll admire the burnt-red leaves
of a Japanese maple
and commit to painting again.

The dream will arise
from the night within the night,
the inner darkness of endless grief
undisturbed by moonlight
or stars quivering like candles.

We'll create a secret dreamscape
where forgiveness can be plucked
like an apple from a tree of life
and bruises are simply lyrics
to an old blues song.

The traumas, the double-binds,
the abuses of childhood
will shimmer like jewels of resilience
in your blue eyes.

I toss and turn, unable to sleep or dream.
The battered day is shadowless,
the light is spent,
night slowly creaks and closes
over your life.

I rage at your death.
Come roar and rush of wind,
silence God's still small voice,
tear brittle leaves from branches,
topple the mightiest oak,
expose ancient gnarled roots.

Rage and rage
until the fury quiets to sheet lightning
blazing and fading
on a distant horizon,

until I humble myself
and live like dust
and a whisper in the wind.

The silence after the storm
feels transcendent.
The moon returns to the sky.

My guilt and shame
for not saving you
unravel into long fly casts
into the silver light
quavering on a still lake.

I pray for the dove to return
after the flood.
Within the stillness
and white-winged hope,
my heart calms
to quiet acceptance.

Your peaceful presence in my heart
teaches me a sad wisdom
of sorrowful loveliness:
Love is a bridge to healing grief.

The Monterey Cypress Tree

I hike the Cypress Grove Trail
in Pointe Lobos State Natural Reserve.
The path opens onto an ocean vista,
azure waives pounding
against weathered sandstone.

A lone Monterey Cypress
clings to the craggy cliff,
stubborn exposed roots holding firm
in the fissures of ancient rock.

Growing up, Sis endured alone
the bellow and brawn of Dad's raging storms.
The tenacious roots of her paintings
gripped her rugged and ferocious will to survive.

I always thought Sis would struggle
to the end, knowing that redemption
had been reduced to the self-respect
of hopeless resistance and rebellion.

After seeing the empty bottle
beside her bed,
I struggle to keep the memories
and my awe intact.
I dare to ask a forbidden question: why?

In the quiet places of my heart,
I believe mental illness tore her roots
from the ancient rocks,
but she let go with a fight—
her paintings shattered
the eye sockets of God
with images more beautiful than love.

Saved by Small Kindnesses

I can't sleep. It's the anniversary
of my sister's suicide.
She died a recluse, trapped
among hoarded memories of trauma.

I slide out of bed,
my heart drumming a dirge.
I can't get past the echoes
in the almost empty cathedral,
the cold metal of the casket,
the gold cross necklace my mother
carefully placed in the grave.
I believe it was Mom's final cold prayer.

I submerge into grief, whirling,
thrashing, drowning in images.

I gasp for the innocent moments—
tracing her freckles like constellations
as we sat on pastel towels at the beach.

Dark images shove my face
underneath the water.

The terrifying teenage years
I couldn't understand—
her refusal to cry when I touched
the bruises on her arms,
her refusal to smile in family photographs.

I fight to the surface and gasp for air—

we perched on the branches of the Magnolia tree,
safe from our parents shouting on the porch.
She sang to Peter, Paul, and Mary
with a towel wrapped around her wet red hair.
She lived five hundred miles away from home.

More muscular images press my head
below the surface again.

Her precocious artistic talent that drove
me into dreams and nightmares—
her paintings that cut the throat of her role
as the family scapegoat,
her sketches that could gouge out
the eyes of any god.

Her adult death spiral into brilliant madness—
crushing cigarettes in overflowing ashtrays
as she paced and ranted in her painting studio,
burning the skin of the night sky
with a seething cigarette and her flaming mind.

The final relinquishment of resistance—
fading away gently with pills
like fall leaves changing colors,
laying on her bed and gazing
into the devoted eyes of death.

My wife stands beside me,
places her hand on my shoulder
with the assurance of a faith healer.

My lungs open up. I can breathe again.
Her kind touch resuscitates me.

All day it continues,
each kindness reaching toward another.
I walk in the woods behind the house:
a stranger sings to the sunlight
as we pass on the path,
redbuds gift me their heart-shaped leaves,
a deer dips its head to drink from the murmuring creek.

Somehow, these sacred moments find me,
wait for me, determined to keep me
from myself, from the grief
that threatens to submerge me.

At night, my wife and I sit on the couch,
enchanted by the improvisations of a jazz guitar.
I rest my head on her chest and listen
to the flutter of her heart.
I breathe in the kindness of nostalgia
and exhale a cleansing breath,
a calm acceptance of loss.

Visiting My Childhood Beach

My wife and I visit my childhood beach
near Atlantic City.
We stroll the shore in the morning
at high tide. My wife knows me.
She gifts me silence to walk
with the memories of Sis.
I collect unbroken shells, the heirlooms
of Rachel's dreams, in a plastic bag.

My wife stands silently beside me,
our hands laced together.
Between each breath,
wide and deep as resurrection,
we rest in a caesura of eternity.

In the afternoon, my wife and I return to the beach.
Sis and I used to prance over the hot sand
with a yellow umbrella and plant it near
the water to stake our claim to our favorite spot.

Mom slathered Sis' fair skin with suntan lotion.
I counted the freckles on my sister's face.
Sis and I squinted, watching the gulls
flame in the noonday sun.

Dad, being a Navy man, loved the ocean.
The lifeguards let him row the wooden
lifeguard boat over the rough waves.

The beach was the only place
we felt safe with Dad.

Years of pain receded to low tide.
We dared to touch our father
in the ocean, clinging to his legs
like barnacles attached to the hull
of a massive ship as he taught us
to ride the gentle waves.

We depended on his strength,
trusted
his glistening body,
waited
for him to pick the perfect breaker,
waited
for the rise of the water,
the jostle, surge, and tumble of joy.

For a moment, we were greater
than our fear and hatred.

Mom read a book under the umbrella
and doted on Sis, insisting she apply
more sunscreen after each dip in the ocean.
The attention was almost too much to bear.

The entire family rode bikes
on the boardwalk to an outside
festival in Atlantic City.

Mom and Dad led the way,
past the stone convent,
the ramps to the casinos,
the storm clouds lost at sea.

Dad won a kite at a festival game,
and we watched it hover and dip
into the magenta beauty of twilight.
As the kite scraped along the sand,
I grew sad. I didn't want the day to end.

That night, the full moon watched wide-eyed
as Sis and I savored the day
and cherished the miracles that could never
be beaten out of us by life.

Now, my wife and I sit on a towel
as dusk closes down the day.
I share with her those childhood
days touched by paradise.

My voice cracks, a lifetime of pain
and happiness seep from my heart
into the fragile words.

Searching for Forgiveness

My father and sister
are buried six feet apart,
names and sins
blurred by green patina
covering their bronze grave markers.

I settle for a diluted comfort
in memories degraded by nostalgia,
remembering the summer days Dad
taught us to ride waves at the beach.

I gather heirlooms of Rachel's life
in beautiful boxes.
But I can't forgive what I can't forget,
like the fearful nights Sis marked
the low-water marks
on Dad's whiskey bottles.

I don't know who to forgive.

Our father for bludgeoning
Rachel's childhood unrecognizable?

Our mother for covering
the bruises with make-up?

God for breaking a bent
and damaged reed?

Me, the blonde, blue-eyed
chosen one, for stealing
our mother's love?

Sis, my protector and savior,
for refusing to hang on a cross?
Her death abandoned me
to a brutal world.

After all the years,
I seek to let Sis go,
to nestle into that love
embedded in grief and suffering.

But forgiveness still seems elusive,
like starlings darting into branches.
I wait for God to touch my loneliness.
I wait for Him, like a kintsugi master,
to brush the lacquer of the golden hour
over my shattered heart.

Coming to Terms with Our Father

There are so many things I wish
I could tell Rachel since she died.
I am trying to come to terms
with our father without cheap forgiveness.
I am trying to stare directly
into the eyes of the trauma
and come out healed on the other side.

Heavy footsteps in the hallway.
I turn off the nightlight,
feeling erased in the darkness.
I'm invisible, I don't exist.

Creak of the door.
I clutch my baseball glove.
I need Mom.
I'm a baby Rhesus monkey
clinging to a wire mesh mother.

A silhouette haunts the bedroom.
I can't close my eyes.
Mom says ghosts don't exist.
I wish my father was dead.

Silence creeps toward the bed.
Maybe this is a dream.
Fear strangles my screams.
All I can hear is the pounding
of my heart deep
within the silo of my chest.

Smell of whiskey on his breath.
Come God,
like a comic book superhero,
strike him dead, slay him
with a miracle.

Swirl of time and space,
torn shirt, a guttural curse.
He has stolen the wrath of God.
I'm bad. I shouldn't have
broken the vase, tracked mud
in the house, talked back to him.

His meaty hand squeezes my arm.
Jerk and pull. I'm a ragdoll.
God, where are you?
Isn't your heart breaking?

Lash of my father's belt,
welts on flesh, scars of shame.
I shake my fist at God.
Why do you look away?
Or do you watch
like an impotent voyeur?
I'm sinful, unredeemable.

Years later,
Dad lies in a nursing home,
wrath muted to fear in his eyes.

Regrets fracture my heart.
If only we had gone fishing together.
Forgiveness would be nothing more
than the catch and release
of a trophy trout back
into the depths of a blue lake.

Death suffocates his breathing.
Tears plead for compassion.
I want to look away, curse his name.

I choose to struggle against the raging current.
My father has been reduced
to his raw humanity. He is only a man.
My lips brush against his wrinkles.
I am loved. I am a child of God.

The Repetition of Grief

I lie on a pastel blanket on a beach
near Atlantic City,
watching gulls burn
in the golden fire of the sun,
listening to the waves
crashing, crashing, crashing,
a rhythmic ritual of grief,
God is dead, God is dead, God is dead.

The sweltering heat melts
my dark memories and sins like tar.
My soul is naked and sick in the light.
I have never touched the hem
of a savior's garment, felt the electric
healing power of a suffering savior.

And the waves are punishing the shore,
pounding, pounding, pounding,
all have sinned and fallen short,
all have sinned and fallen short,
all have sinned and fallen short.

My transistor radio describes
the latest shrapnel scarring society.
I fear God has given the world
over to evil;
he no longer applauds
his dying creation as good.

He has fled, freed from the cage
of the body of Christ,

leaving behind the broken pieces
of his compassion and love,
shattered shells washed ashore.
And the waves,
those terrible crashing waves
of eternal mourning,
are wailing, wailing, wailing.

My heart rocks with the ritualized grief,
but I can't bury my dead.
I have watched my father, mother, and sister
die in the absence of God.
And the waves are crying out with a guttural voice
of deep anguish.
My God, why have you forsaken me?
My God, why have you forsaken me?
My God, why have you forsaken me?

Dementia slowly devoured
my mother's lifelong faith.
God withered in her mind.
She died fumbling with her rosary
without knowing why.
And the waves are hammering doubts.
The idea of God is rootless.
The idea of God is rootless.
The idea of God is rootless.

My sister died insane, a scapegoat
driven into the wilderness by our father.

In her final days, she painted God
with brilliant delusions,
danced with angels
singing on an unplugged radio.
And the waves
are roaring, roaring, roaring,
at the empty delusions of God.

My father died in a sterile hospital room,
his chest heaving on a ventilator machine.
The crosscurrents of my grief
kept me from crying.
I hated him.

I had seen too much on the nights
he stirred his anger into a whiskey on the rocks
and slurred or bellowed my sister's name.
But the idealized father wouldn't die.
He taught me to find the perfect fishing hole.
And the waves are pleading like Esau,
weeping, weeping, weeping,
bless me too my father,
bless me too my father,
bless me too my father.

My father and I never talked
the night of his death.
I watched the final flatline of forgiveness.
And the waves sound
like my father's heaving chest,

surrendering, surrendering, surrendering,
to death,
it is finished,
it is finished,
it is finished.

I lie on my pastel blanket,
fearing a world without grace,
without the compassion of God.
The gray gulls veer upward
and transfigure golden
in the glow of the sun.
And I listen to the waves
rejoicing, rejoicing, rejoicing,
I am the great I am,
I am the great I am,
I am the great I am.

I close my eyes, let my imagination
take wing on the wind.
I picture Rachel's soul leaving this earth,
surfacing in heaven,
her pulse racing with eternity,
her freckles and blue eyes
gleaming untainted
like sea glass
washed up on a new shore.

Cool Fire

power shut off, five candles
flickering in my sister's hovel
long past a timeless midnight,

haughty, a daredevil
chain-smoking
on the edge of death,

she carved at the darkness
with her blazing, unfiltered
Camel cigarette,

she glowered
at a memory of our father,
prayers iced over my heart,

she thawed, wept,
we stilled,
listened,

angels played a haunting
silent riff
on her unplugged radio,

and yet, the melody
lingered underneath the silence,
a sacred liturgy of insanity,

the sound still moves me now
to write a poem
that will make someone cry,

to trace the initials we carved
years ago in the twisted oak tree
in the backyard,

if I remembered the entire song
I'd know who I am,
look my wife in the eyes

and tell her I love her,
release my anger,
forgive my worst enemy,

the forgotten melody
persists, insists,
resurfaces,

in the shiver of my daughter
splashing
into a cold pool,

in the star-shower
of wishes
on a camping trip to Wyoming,

only to submerge again
under the clamor and press
of an un-enchanted life,

I grieved the lost dream-tune
until my daughter taught me
another fragment last night,

I read her the story of Meshach
and the fiery furnace,
she hummed

quietly,
and sang an improvised riff,
Meshach danced in cool fire,

now that's a sound
that will steal the show
in Blind Willie's Jazz Club.

From the Psalter of Love and Grief

For so long, I feared God
when rumbling storm clouds
shredded into dark silence
against distant mountain cliffs.
I hated Him when Sis scorched
and burned her future.

I viewed Rachel's abuse
and scapegoat role
as God's responsibility, his shadow side,
his wrath, his original sin.
I shaped God into the image of Dad.
I couldn't love the God I created.

But grief is a patient teacher,
allowing truth to slowly
seep into my heart.

I now know that evil exists.
Sis and I weren't nurtured on love;
we were raised on evil.
During Rachel's childhood,
that malevolent force
manifested itself in Dad's balled fist,
the bellow and brawn of his storms,
the vicious thunderclaps of his abuse.

Evil slaughtered Rachel's beauty,
disfigured her self-image,
trapped her in a self-destructive madness.

I am no longer afraid of God's punishment.
On the beach where my sister
and I used to walk,
I rejoice, listening
to the first thunderous waves
that drummed the world into being
with a wild and untamed holiness.

I thank God for tempering
His primitive power with love.
When I hated and blamed Him
for Rachel's suffering,
a patient grief taught me that even anger
is a relationship with Him,
a rope pulled taut and knotted,
tying me to His love and forgiveness.

Grief has taught me to nestle into God's motherlove.
God swaddles me in a blanket made from the Psalms
and comforts me like a child at a mother's breast.

God's tenderness is a breeze sweeping over
the top of pines like a drum brush
swishing softly across a drumhead.
God's motherlove could never bruise Sis.

My grief teaches me to love Sis
with an eternal perspective.
Death cannot separate her from God.

Her name is engraved
on the palm of God's hand.
God's motherlove will never forget her.

Grief has taught me intimacy with God.
I follow a Savior
who had calluses on his hands and feet,
dirt and dust on his sandals.
He hung on a tree, raised between two thieves.

I even dare to call God Father.
As I returned home after my wandering,
He flung His arms around me
and shouted:
Welcome home, my son.
I have been waiting for you.

Creation sings hallelujah.
The blue trumpets of morning glory
open with praise for morning's light.

I want to share with Sis that my heart
is humble, shaped like a manger,
and my poetry sings hallelujah,
rejoicing in the triumph
of an empty tomb.

Go in Peace

At first, after Rachel's cremation,
there were brief moments my grief
dared to look directly into the sun.
My sister died alone,
thin and bent as a crooked walking stick,
a recluse secluded in madness,
hating herself with whiskey.

The mailman smelled Rachel's
decaying body through the mail slot.
Sis had been decomposing
in a barren bedroom
desolate as charnel ground.

***

Sungazing at suicide
burned my retinas,
left me blind and groping
at the disfigured faces
of hope and love.

To cope, I dove inward
below the tears and grief
into light-saturated memories
where Sis continued to survive,
to set her jaw
against the cruelties of childhood.

I nestled into a nest of warm memories.

On the weekends, when Dad was far away
doing volunteer work,
hammering nails at a construction site
in Elijah, Georgia
and listening to Johnny Cash
on his truck radio during the breaks,
we breathed deep-lunged in the garden,
playing like angels with shafts of light.

We thrived among songbirds,
birdbaths, water spraying
from a garden hose, the creak
of a wooden swing,
the relaxed presence of Mom.

Sis was fresh and beautiful, blooming
in her new sundress.
I chased her around the white azaleas,
lassoing her innocence with laughter.

Mom wore a floppy straw hat
and looked carefree and silly
as she planted green Hosta
and white teacup roses.
Her smile was broad and easy,
like a hammock stretched
between two oak trees.
Her love was shaped like shears.
She pruned our wild exuberance
into bright joy.

Too soon, the light bled into twilight
like Jesus sweating blood in Gethsemane.
Too soon, dusk closed over the light,
slowly like a coffin lid.
Trees grieved the death of their shadows.
We retreated into the house,
our bunker, our cave of hiding.

Mom prepared dinner in the kitchen,
the pots and pans clattered like chains,
her shoulders slumped
under the weight of her cross to bear.
I wanted to cry, she looked like an old lady
being worn down by martyrdom.

I hated the sound of truck wheels
grinding on gravel.
I hated the stiff, muddy boots
Dad abandoned on the front porch.
Rachel said they looked like dead
animals in rigor mortis.

I hated Mom's closed eyes
as she let Dad kiss her on the cheek.
I hated the peeling flowered wallpaper
in the dining room.
I hated Dad as he suffocated silence
at the dinner table.

Suddenly, Sis nonchalantly broke
Dad's death grip on the family.

She lightly held her knife and fork
and began conducting an imaginary
orchestra as she hummed "500 Miles."

Mom's eyes sparkled like newborn stars.
I secretly tapped my foot under the table.
That girl had mastered the art
of living 500 miles away from home.

***

During the early years of my grief,
shame and guilt plagued me.
That was the cost of being the favorite,
the youngest, the only boy.
Remembered moments of preference
felt like weakness and betrayal of Sis.

I collected moments with Dad
like a child hoarding shiny pennies
in his dirty torn pockets.

I was the weak one.
I betrayed Sis.

***

During the first years of my grief,
every song became a lament,
each day was the same,
like Mason jars lined up along a shelf.

I cloistered myself in the blue-walled study
like an ascetic monk.

Rock-bottom, no energy
to tear off my skin—a rank t-shirt
and sweatpants.

The sadness
distorted my face,
bent my spine,
slumped my shoulders,
buckled my knees.

Heavy rain
pounded a dirge on the roof
for the squandered months
raging at the silent
violence of a masculine God,
my sister's bruises
failed to move
His father heart.

Where was the warrior God,
the comforter of the oppressed?
He never lifted
my shaman sister's chin.
The crucifixion never ended.

I resented the beggar's prayer
gathered by God
from the stubble and chaff

of my famine heart:
Grapple with me, Lord,
unhinge my hip,
change my name,
burn a bush with my destiny,
empty a tomb.

I eavesdropped on my family downstairs,
thirsting for the family banter,
the artesian spring bubbling beneath me.
My kids told stories about a math test,
football practice, a new dance step.

I remembered holding court at the table,
weaving stories about game-winning homeruns
and the death penalty case I handled pro bono.

Chairs scraped over linoleum tiles.
Plates clattered.
I didn't have the energy
to play catch with my boy.
Water splashed in the sink.
Silverware clinked.
My daily task was taking out the trash.
Dishwasher hummed.
Voices faded to other rooms.
I closed my eyes.

Why did God hide
in the silent catacombs,

the narrow, winding labyrinths
untouched by light,
deep within the dark, rejected
spaces of my soul?
So many questions,
burnt out torches in the darkness.

***

I was trapped in catacomb darkness.
The only emotion that burned
within me was anger
when I demanded justice.

Justice? Where was justice for Sis?
Buried now side-by-side
with her abuser,
God was nothing but a Bible verse
carved in her blue marble tombstone.

How was I supposed to re-create God as love,
find faith in an imperfect Creator?
Only Sis had the right to forgive our sins.

***

I agonized over how to forgive myself?
I had seen it coming.
Sis could defy Dad,
but she couldn't fight the entire world.

She learned her lovers,
friends, teachers, mentors,
and even her God and baby brother
were all made in the image of Dad.

The weight of betrayal broke her.
I saw the end in her eyes.
They scared me.
Everywhere I looked, I saw her unlit eyes.

How was I supposed to forgive myself?
Sis held my hand
through all of my tears,
all of the years.

I never intervened when I knew.
How was I any different than Mom?
She stayed in her room,
hiding behind her prayers.
I hated her in the morning.
She covered up the bruises with make-up.

How was I any different than God?
He hid behind free will
and watched like an impotent voyeur.
When it came to Sis, God broke his promise.
He bent a bruised reed until it broke.
He snuffed out the smoldering wick in her eyes.

***

Gradually, moments of grace arrested me.
They felt like visitations from Sis.
The experiences were sudden and unexpected,
like a covey of quail flushed from the brush.

Saturday afternoon.
My binoculars offered visions and dreams.
They were miracles, with God healing
my spiritual sight through new lenses.

I stood frozen in a winter landscape,
wind whipping across a frozen lake.
I felt bonded to Rachel by grief,
knowing Sis used to walk
this path with me and share
in the healing of reborn sight.

Canada geese arrived,
obeying the pull of the seasons.
Their black heads, white cheeks,
and long black necks assured me
that beauty still existed.

Wings beat through snowfall,
plunged into sunset's flaming golden hour
above rising black spruce,

disappeared into a memory
of Sis lowering her binoculars,
a miracle gleaming in her tears.

The geese unsettled the water,
abruptly, with sharp startlement
of wing beats. I gazed
past spruce lancing the sunset,
bleeding burgundy on white.
My boots and heartbeat pounded
to the rhythmic miracle of migration.

The lake settled to silence.
I stood within the presence of Sis,
a moment frozen for a season.
I lowered my binoculars
and shared my tears with her.

I pounded gloves together,
unsettled by the unexpected,
out-of-season thawing
of the human heart.

***

Grief slowly revolutionized
my perspective on Rachel's life.
The secret hiding place, the Magnolia tree,
the magic lanterns, and bike rides on the boardwalk
transformed into jewels of resiliency.

Rachel's rebellion against the wrath of God
and the oppressive scapegoat role
became heroic courage.

Her painting suddenly symbolized
more than precocious talent.
Her brushstrokes were a brilliant form
of self-healing and spiritual transcendence.

Her creative moments of happiness
reflected a deep well of love for life
that couldn't be pilfered by Dad,
her righteous anger, or sense of martyrdom.

Her protective presence in my life
was reframed as a gift of God
fragrant as motherlove.

***

I have gazed into the unblinking
stare of death.
I can no longer trudge in the ruts
of my ordinary routines.

I want to step outside my drab context
and leave the beaten path to find
the perfect sunrise.

I want to hike the Camino de Santiago,
listen to Kamasi Washington blow night rhythms
on his saxophone at the Village Vanguard,
spend a month in Paris learning French,
explore the cobbled streets of Montmartre
to find the colors of Renoir
and the savage spirit of Josephine Baker.

I want to grasp trauma as a chisel
to carve something beautiful out of the rough
unfinished stone of suffering.

Most of all, I want to pick up my pen
and grieve in poetry,
releasing the suffering into healing words.

***

My grief over Rachel's death
has deepened my love of life.
The awareness of death
turns memories into heirlooms,
the future into crossroads, life lessons, and legacies,
and the present into veins of gold, grace, and gifts.
The inevitability of death replaces the boredom
and repetition of immortality with the live wire
electricity and jolt of present moments.

Death motivates me to break generational sins,
to polish the tarnished past with integrity,
to define the meaning and measure of a good life.

Death spotlights the shimmering diamonds
of the present,
the brushstrokes of the golden hour on the horizon,
the innocence of snow falling soft as grace.

Death is a master of paradoxes and surprises,
turning the terror of crucifixion and tears of blood
into the context for empty tombs and resurrection.

The deep cracks of sin in a broken world
allow God to create the unexpected beauty
of a kintsugi vessel.

The grief over the suicide of my sister
debrides my life of shallow happiness
and serves as a bridge to acceptance and peace.

Death blows on the gambling dice and rolls life events
that feel like fate, but the retrospective of old age
stitches those moments into a beautiful prayer shawl.

***

I am old. I have buried my mother, father, and Sis.
I have reconciled with death
and lived past the fear of death.

Many red and gold autumn leaves
have drifted down the ever-changing river
of my life.

I have discovered one thing:
my love has learned to embrace suffering
and outlast grief.

I visit the cemetery every month
and sit on a marble bench underneath two oak trees.
The branches write words of forgiveness in the dirt
with the calligraphy of shade.

A river runs beside the cemetery.
Aspen trees line the bank,
their leaves tremble
with the slightest breeze,
attuned to the breath of the Spirit.

I walk to the river and take off my shoes.
The cool water clasps my ankles.

I release the memories of Sis
into the river. They drift downriver
with the autumn leaves
and disappear into the twilight.

I smile, realizing Sis was always
the spiritual one.
Her soul escaped a tormented world
long ago on a journey to find a new home.

I finally let her go in peace.

A Festival of Lights

My sister lived her life
500 miles away from home,
tossing cigarettes
into an incense burner,
reducing her trauma to ashes,
listening to protest music
strummed on acoustic guitars.

She wrote her life
on her flesh
with henna tattoos
and adorned her independence
from the scapegoat role
with hoop earrings
and twenty-four-carat gold.

She settled into a rented apartment
at Carnegie Mellon
before insanity and addiction
drove her into a wilderness
filled with whitewashed bones.
God never adopted her
like Hagar,
never dug wells for her
in the dryness of the desert.

She lived the rest of her life
with an empty skin of water.
I felt helpless, unable to sustain her,
unable to play God for her.
She taught me to shake my fist
at earthly and heavenly fathers.

I miss her.
At night, I trace the constellations
as if they were her childhood freckles.
It gives me comfort
that she is so far above this world.

When I tend my garden,
I remember her as a teenager
blooming in a new sundress.
I grieve with smiles
rather than tears.

She is near to me,
free of torment,
whispering to me
like the wind
billowing a sail,
like a soft breeze
quivering in aspen leaves.

Her suicide is the reason
I live beyond the fear of death.
She is my Festival of Lights.
I decorate lanterns with candles
and whispered prayers
and release them downriver.
I watch them drift,
perhaps toward a place
she can call home.

Ascending into the Presence of God

As a child, Rachel taught me
to climb an old Magnolia tree,
branch by branch.
We climbed until we felt safe
and transcended our pain.

After Rachel's suicide, her presence
teaches me to climb the spiritual crags
and rough places,
the great mountains of death and sorrow.
We travel light and empty handed, smiling.

Sis has taught me to become
a climber of cliffs,
mindful moment by mindful moment,
rising from rocky and barren tribulations
to secret and sacred heights,
quiet moment by quiet moment,
inhaling the thin air of revival,
silent moment by silent moment,
ascending toward the presence of God.

After our ascent of the rugged
spiritual mountains, Sis and I
lose ourselves in the heights,
far above memories and traumas.

We exist beyond paths
near the untouched cliffs
of rocks and scree,
searching for a sacred place
where an untamed God roars.

We kneel beside a rivulet
born from retreating snow,
cup our hands and drink the water,
tasting the cold beginning
of creeks and rivers.

From our perch on the crags
we watch our lives unfurl
to the glorious end.
We take flight,
freely veering and wheeling,
riding the wind, distant and powerful,
like hawks kiting above the madness
of our beautifully wrecked lives,
untouched by the traumas
that used to break our wings.

About the Author

Theodore McDowell is a retired attorney who grew up with his older sister within the family crucible of abuse, alcoholism, and mental illness. Mr. McDowell's adult years were also shaped by trauma, including the death of his sister by suicide, addiction, mental illness, and a traumatic brain injury.

This poetic memoir explores McDowell's relationship with his sister. Within the family of origin, his sister was his protector, shaman, guardian angel, and best friend. Her death by suicide as an adult was a significant loss in Theodore's life. The poems explore McDowell's grief and healing from the loss. Ultimately, he finds meaning and hope in his sister's beautiful and creative life.

McDowell has previously published five additional poetry books. *Yearning for Human Touch* is a collection of poems and short stories on trauma. *Evenings on the Edge of Death* addresses the traumas within his family of origin and the heartbreaking death of his mother from dementia. *Excavating the Cruelty of Memories* focuses on Theodore's adult traumas, such as addiction, a traumatic brain injury, mental illness, and periods of living on the streets of downtown Atlanta. Finally, *Drinking from God's Well* highlights the healing, reconciliation, and hope related to these traumas through the grace of God. Finally, *Stained Glass Tainted by Dementia* explores Mr. McDowell's relationship with his mother as she experienced the long goodbye of dementia and his grieving and healing process after her death. The book also examines dementia from the perspective of individuals with dementia, family members, and caretakers.

McDowell currently resides in Atlanta, Georgia and is married with five adult children and seven grandchildren scattered across the United States.

About the Author

www.ingramcontent.com/pod-product-compliance
Lightning Source LLC
La Vergne TN
LVHW090612110826
845146LV00001B/363